Once Upon A Dream

Sleep Tight

Edited By Lynsey Evans

First published in Great Britain in 2024 by:

Young Writers
Remus House
Coltsfoot Drive
Peterborough
PE2 9BF
Telephone: 01733 890066
Website: www.youngwriters.co.uk

All Rights Reserved
Book Design by Ashley Janson
© Copyright Contributors 2024
Softback ISBN 978-1-83685-052-6
Printed and bound in the UK by BookPrintingUK
Website: www.bookprintinguk.com
YB0MA0075A

FOREWORD

Welcome Reader, to a world of dreams.

For Young Writers' latest competition, we asked our writers to dig deep into their imagination and create a poem that paints a picture of what they dream of, whether it's a make-believe world full of wonder or their aspirations for the future.

The result is this collection of fantastic poetic verse that covers a whole host of different topics. Let your mind fly away with the fairies to explore the sweet joy of candy lands, join in with a game of fantasy football, or you may even catch a glimpse of a unicorn or another mythical creature. Beware though, because even dreamland has dark corners, so you may turn a page and walk into a nightmare!

Whereas the majority of our writers chose to stick to a free verse style, others gave themselves the challenge of other techniques such as acrostics and rhyming couplets. We also gave the writers the option to compose their ideas in a story, so watch out for those narrative pieces too!

Each piece in this collection shows the writers' dedication and imagination – we truly believe that seeing their work in print gives them a well-deserved boost of pride, and inspires them to keep writing, so we hope to see more of their work in the future!

CONTENTS

Abu Bakr Al-Ihsaan Academy, Walsall
Haziqah Yousaf (11) — 1

Avonwood Primary School, Bournemouth
Alexandra Tees (7) — 2
Khadijah Merdaci (8) — 3

Bamford Primary School, Bamford
Stanley Locking-Fair (9) — 4

Barlestone CE Primary School, Barlestone
Rhoswen Hughes (9) — 5

Beckfoot Priestthorpe Primary School, Bingley
Amber-Rose Auker (11) — 6

Bishop Ellis Catholic Voluntary Academy, Leicester
Krish Neetin (9) — 7
Alice Debicka (9) — 8

Bridge Integrated Primary School, Banbridge
Sienna Beggs (10) — 9
Katie Martin (10) — 10
Jack McCullough (10) — 11
Ella-Rose Liggett (10) — 12
Carter Wilson (10) — 13
Tyler Grant (10) — 14
Tommy Martin (10) — 15

Bromley High Junior School, Bickley
Charlotte Okoli (8) — 16

Cherrywood Community Primary School, Farnborough
Daisy Allen (9) — 17
Kayden Ray-Leitch (10) — 18
Destiny Lemon (10) — 19
Alice Wray (10) — 20
Mailee Karim (10) — 21
Jamie Milner (10) — 22
Aevan Thapa Magar (9) — 23

Chichester Free School, Chichester
George Outen (10) — 24

Crondall Primary School, Crondall
Saoirse Crean (10) — 25
Rupert Love (9) — 26

Downsend School, Leatherhead

Sebastian Salter (9)	27
Isabella Fernandez-Pell (9)	28
Abigail Young (9)	29
Joseph Muller (8)	30
Ellie Dada (9)	31
Mae Harverson (8)	32
Albie Lambert (9)	33
Ruben Lovell-Djordjevic (9)	34
Beatrice Woolnough (9)	35
Ray Cummings (9)	36
Leo Ling (9)	37

Drove Primary School, Swindon

Sarah Locham (8)	38
Khadijah Mohamed (10)	39

Drumahoe Primary School, Drumahoe

Erin Davies (9)	40
Mollie Frazer (8)	42
Brooke Bradley (9)	43
Emilie King (9)	44
Zac McGeady (10)	45
Megan Hetherington (9)	46
Brooke McCready (10)	47
Charlie Hepburn (9)	48
Layla Neely (11)	49
Eli Hunter (8)	50
Lexie Mitchell (9)	51
Callum Campbell (9)	52

Etz Chaim Jewish Primary School, Mill Hill

Tamar Raanan Djamal (9)	53
Louis Blank (9)	54

Glebe House School, Hunstanton

Oren Neidle (10)	55
Jack Nicholas (10)	56

Glusburn Community Primary School, Glusburn

Orla Lewis (10)	57
Nina Moore (10)	58
Ava Bond (10)	59

Goldbeaters Primary School, Edgware

Andrea Tertelici (8)	60
Naba Asghar (9)	61
Nicole Kabuye (9)	62

Grange CE Primary School, Grange-Over-Sands

Drew Lord (10)	63
Reyn Gray (10)	64
Rowan Gray (10)	65

Hafod Primary School, Swansea

Nadim Al Mousa (10)	66

Hall Green Primary School, West Bromwich

Esme-Rose Harris (9)	67

Holy Cross Catholic Primary School, Liverpool

Akiva Jewel Devanada (9)	68
Alberta Edosa (9)	69

Holy Ghost Catholic Primary School, Wandsworth

Rebecca Laker Lebeja (8)	70
Patrick Keenan (9)	71
Sophie Russell (8)	72
Carolina Isaza de la Rocha (8)	73

Kingswood Primary School, Lambeth

Reeda Faizi (8) — 74

Lapal Primary School, Halesowen

Takudzwa Mukozho-Sonwil (10) — 75
Sophie Anderson (10) — 76
Maisie Williams (10) — 78
Hashim Ahmed (10) — 80
Larry Logan (10) — 81

Lea Forest Primary Academy, Kitts Green

Scarlett Du-Cille (8) — 82
Laila Peace (10) — 83
Lyla Black (7) — 84

Loxdale Primary School, Bilston

Adebayo Mandela Soyelu (8) — 85

Meryfield Primary School, Borehamwood

Daria Bargaoanu (10) — 86
Elsie (10) — 87
Krish Singh (10) — 88
Radhika Tanwar (8) — 89
Brooklyn (9) — 90
Teddy Shuttleworth (10) — 91
Dhrumi Patel (9) — 92
Elisa (8) — 93

Nether Edge Primary School, Sheffield

Amelia Khan (10) — 94

Newtown CE (VC) Primary School, Gosport

Josie Slaler-Winter (10) — 95
Oscar Usher (10) — 96

Norfolk House School, Edgbaston

Ismael Abbas (10) — 97

Oak Lodge Primary School, West Wickham

Sergi Tasali (9) — 98
Maisie Willsmore (10) — 99

Pontarddulais Primary School, Pontarddulais

Charlie Carew (9) — 100
William Stevens (9) — 101
Jake Gabe (9) — 102

Provost Williams CofE Primary School, Coventry

Ruby-Mae Evans (9) — 103
Olivia Summers (8) — 104

Rackenford CE (VA) Primary School, Rackenford

Kaitlyn Martin (11) — 106
Rosie Webber (9) — 107

Sacred Heart Catholic School, Thornton-Cleveleys

Penny Clarke (8) — 108

Shobdon Primary School, Leominster

Chiara Lock (12) — 109
Saffire Crick (10) — 110

St Bede's Catholic Academy, Ashby

Sienna Dent-Sheath (13)	111
Keeley Woodmansey (12)	112

St Clare's Catholic Primary School, Bradford

Azim Sidiqi (9)	113

St Edward's CE Academy, Leek

Chloe Hale (12)	114
Oscar Budd (12)	115
Gabe Ager (12)	116
Jack Siwiec (12)	117

St James' CE Primary School, West End

Felicity Robinson (9)	118

St John's CE Primary School, Keele

Alfie Li (10)	119
Oleena Kabbekadaurs (9)	120
Olivia Abbotts (10)	121
Ella-Rose Richardson (9)	122
Aarha Haider (10)	123

St Joseph's Catholic Primary School, Kirkham

Renee Wilcox (8)	124

St Mary's Catholic Primary School, Preston

Bonnie Rees (10)	125
Leo Arnold (9)	126
Charlie Roberts (9)	127

St Mary's CE Primary School, Barnsley

Umut Uras Gokpinar (9)	128
Ella Knighton (9)	129
Adeline Moore (9)	130
Rafe Trickett (8)	131
Carla Wilson (8)	132
James Long (9)	133
Charlie Dutton (9)	134

St Matthew's CE Primary School, Blackmoor

Seb Jarocki (9)	135

St Modwen's Catholic Primary School, Burton-On-Trent

JJ Finnegan (10)	136
Raphael Chacko (10)	137

St Peter's Catholic Primary School, Dagenham

Ariah Nable-Russell (8)	138

St Peter's CE Primary School, Chorley

Orla O'Dwyer (9)	139

Staynor Hall Community Primary Academy, Selby

Joseph Dean (8)	140
Janusz Bowes (8)	142
Ruby Liddle (9)	143
Jason Samson (8)	144
Patrick Bowes (8)	145

Tany's Dell Primary School & Nursery, Harlow

Holly Bonner (9)	146
Chace Brown (8)	147
Davina Bonsu (9)	148
Jacob Fisk (8)	149
Erin Pennell (9)	150
Ivaylo Todorov (9)	151
Alyssa Gibbons (9)	152
Sana Sakak (9)	153

The Friary School, Lichfield

Danielle Abbott (13)	154

Three Bridges Primary School, Three Bridges

Zhen Labandero (8)	155
Theodore C (8)	156
Asiya Islam (8)	157
Daria Dadu (8)	158
Daniel James Goncalves (8)	159
Adrian Fernandes (8)	160
Ricky Bindela (8)	161

Upton Cross Primary School, Plaistow

Mariah Syed (9)	162
Sheyzda Uddin (10)	163
Ibrahim Ansar (10)	164

Victory Primary School, Portsmouth

Spencer Rolfe (10)	165

Weston Turville Church Of England School, Weston Turville

Ralph Boon (7)	166

Whitchurch Primary School & Nursery, Stanmore

Estrella Dada (8)	167

Woodcock Hill Primary School, Northfield

Marayha Hunter-Holness (9)	168
Howaida El Sanousi (9)	169

Woodhouse Primary Academy, Quinton

Nibras Ibrahem (8)	170

Woolaston Primary School, Lydney

Monty Lewis (10)	171

Yohden Primary School, Peterlee

Jack Clarke Wandlass (8)	172

Ysgol Y Plas, Colwyn Bay

Teddie Davies (10)	173

THE CREATIVE WRITING

Lost In The Forest

Once upon a time,
I had a dream.
I was with my friends,
Eating ice cream.
But suddenly, *whoosh!*
A gust of wind came,
Blowing me and my friends away.
Lost in a forest,
Frightened and scared,
I got up and saw a growling bear.
Teeth baring,
And brown fur.
I ran for my life,
Gasping for breath.
I tripped on a log,
Thinking this would be the end.
But suddenly, I woke up in bed.

Haziqah Yousaf (11)
Abu Bakr Al-Ihsaan Academy, Walsall

Bowy

B owy the black cat.
L exi is Bowy's owner.
A cat called Lala is Bowy's best friend.
C uddles are Bowy's thing.
K hadigha, Bowy's mouse, is fun to play with.

C ats are my favourite animal.
A bed is Bowy's favourite place to sleep.
T ea time for Bowy.

Alexandra Tees (7)
Avonwood Primary School, Bournemouth

Midnight

M idnight, I hear noises
 I nside the house
D angerous clowns are all around me
N o mum or dad here to say there's no sound
 I n the bed alone
G rouching down under the blanket
H ear mum and dad say it's alright
T hen I fall asleep with sleepy eyes.

Khadijah Merdaci (8)
Avonwood Primary School, Bournemouth

Just A Dream

In my dream last night
I was in a room with red candlelight
I was all alone
I just wanted to be at home
I got stuck in the room
And looked out the window
And saw the moon
When I woke up, I was no longer stuck
It was just a dream.

Stanley Locking-Fair (9)
Bamford Primary School, Bamford

Bedtime Stories

I snuggle down with warm sleepy eyes,
I get cosy with my PJs on.
The soft soothing sound of the storyteller's voice,
Travels through my ear and into my mind,
Leading my imagination into strange new places,
I am yet to discover.
My mind is full, my senses tingle with joy.
I embrace them like the sweet taste of cherries.
I drift off slowly to sleep,
Like a feather floating in the air.
Bedtime stories are the best!
They truly let me rest.
Good night.

Rhoswen Hughes (9)
Barlestone CE Primary School, Barlestone

The Silhouette

The silhouette! It lurks in the woods!
The silhouette! It craves the taste of blood!
The silhouette! No one expects it to come!
The silhouette! Don't think, just run!
The silhouette! Will bleed you dry!
The silhouette! Don't let it hear you cry!
The silhouette! Turns everything dark!
The silhouette! Will hear even the smallest crack of bark!
The silhouette! When you hide, don't breathe!
The silhouette! If it hears you, it won't leave!

Amber-Rose Auker (11)
Beckfoot Priestthorpe Primary School, Bingley

The Story Of How My Rocket Went Out Of Control

In my dreams every night, I have a dream that I can fly into space with my friends in my rocket.
Then suddenly my rocket went out of control.
I didn't know what was going on in my dreams.
So I landed on the moon with you.
When I landed on the moon I discovered I was with you.
When I was done discovering I went back to the Earth with you.
When I arrived I saw my parents on land so I went home with them.

Krish Neetin (9)
Bishop Ellis Catholic Voluntary Academy, Leicester

The Adventure

In my dream, the stars led me and my friend Aaron from our ship.
We jumped out with a flip onto the stars to Mars.
Bang!
We hit Mars and back to the stars again.
We felt amazing because we hit a galaxy and the stars fell into a pit.
We flipped and clipped back to the ship.
I heard the stars clanging together as we fell into the pit full of stars.
This dream will always be kept.

Alice Debicka (9)
Bishop Ellis Catholic Voluntary Academy, Leicester

Untitled

R ough as can be when I wake up, it's as dark as a pea.
O h to wake up in the middle of the night leaves you with a bit of a fright.
Y ou're so stupid for falling for my trap, next time I'll maybe leave you in a flat.
A ll alone and on your own.
L oved by plenty, hated by many.

C aring for those who need a laugh.
L ife itself can be a draft.
O nly facepaint and makeup will do, make sure to add a clown nose too.
W hat a surprise, seeing a clown at a party will meet your demise.
N ow it's time to stop playing games and run or you'll meet your end, sadly it's come.

Sienna Beggs (10)
Bridge Integrated Primary School, Banbridge

Six Nations

All I can hear is
The yelling of the crowds
Cheering or booing us
My feet are like superglue
My feet stuck to the ground
I stare at my teammates walking forward
Come on feet, *move*, I think
I'm standing there humiliated
I finally get my feet moving
We start the game.

It's off to a bad start
We're down fifteen-nil
Oh no, they've scored again!
Twenty-nil, oh come on!
We need to make a comeback,
I'm not very hopeful,
Bundee the centre
Passes to me
My big moment
I run straight, "No!" I say.

Katie Martin (10)
Bridge Integrated Primary School, Banbridge

Abandoned House With Monsters

One day I stumbled upon a building whilst jogging,
I looked into the darkness, then I started running,
The reason I started running was because of a creepy smile,
After I got out, I ran as long as a mile,
A few days later, I went back to the beach,
But the creepy smile was still waiting to get me.

I was frightened but I wanted to see the rest of him,
When I saw more monsters come out, then I got attacked,
But not even for a few seconds, I was already taken
But I woke up in my home, safe in my bed.

Jack McCullough (10)
Bridge Integrated Primary School, Banbridge

I Love Cheerleading

C heering with my besties
H appy on the hot, sandy beach
E xcited to do new stunts and tricks
E specially our flips and kicks
R unning and jumping in the sky
L etting all your worries die
E veryone cheering for us so loud
A nd we are making everyone proud
D ancing with our pom-poms in the air
I love cheering and I don't care
N othing can stop us from wanting to dance
G et on your feet and give it a chance.

Ella-Rose Liggett (10)
Bridge Integrated Primary School, Banbridge

Noises

A bomb goes *boom*,
A car goes *brum*,
A calf goes *moo*,
A song goes *bop* to the *beat*,
A pig goes *oink*,
And when I got hit, I said, "That was a loud *doink* and a *dink*."
Someone said, "He might be dead!"

Carter Wilson (10)
Bridge Integrated Primary School, Banbridge

The Clowns

Clowns are scary and funny
Like no other
They are outrageously destructive
With their blade-sharp teeth
Now something still scares me
So I won't go to any clown show.

Tyler Grant (10)
Bridge Integrated Primary School, Banbridge

Untitled

We were playing Real Madrid
We were one-nil down
And we needed to score
About three minutes later, I scored
I and my team celebrated a lot.

Tommy Martin (10)
Bridge Integrated Primary School, Banbridge

The Creepy Dreamland Forest

N othing has prepared me for this strange land I see
I take one more step and it's louder, you see
G lancing left then right, all I see are trees
H ow did I get here? I hope it's a joke
T *hud*, something moves, oh no, it's back
M y worst fear has arrived - a creepy zombie
A run starts, faster and faster and faster
R un! Zombies run so quick, well, in this story they do
E erie eyes fade as light comes again
S oon, I am safe, at home in bed

And no more zombies running around.

Charlotte Okoli (8)
Bromley High Junior School, Bickley

Never-Ending Corridors

N ever-ending corridors popped up in my dream,
E very ghoul, zombie, vampire made me scream,
V icious vampires bare their razor-sharp teeth,
E very vampire made my helpful heart miss a beat,
R ows and rows of doors and lifts,

E normous harbours filled with blood-dripping skips,
N ightmares always feel so real
D esire that I can never reach makes it feel unreal,
I n this world, there is
N o life except for your soul,
G etting closer and closer until morning...

C loser and closer until morning,
O h! Finally an escape from this brain boggling,
R eally close until dawn,
R un! Run! There is a ghoul!
I n through a door and into a hall,
D oors! Doors! Which one do I choose?
O pen this door! No! Not that
doo **R,** sleep has been broken!
S afe at last!

Daisy Allen (9)
Cherrywood Community Primary School, Farnborough

Dreamland

Dreams are always within my mind, they just come at night,
Children playing happily on rainbows,
Dragons rapidly racing above my head,
Whispering animals filling the air,
Running rivers full of glowing stars and swimming swans.

Dreams are like clouds that are always floating around,
Everlasting in my mind,
A dream is like a book taking you on a fascinating journey,
A dream is like a never-ending puzzle blocking brain signals.

In Dreamland, you will hear the hushed whispers,
Parents reading stories to their dozing children,
The dark night sky is like the minds of sleeping children.

Kayden Ray-Leitch (10)
Cherrywood Community Primary School, Farnborough

The Land Of Dreams

At night, there are magical creatures sprinting,
Through the calm, breezy air.
At night, hushed whispers of parents reading to
Dozing children

As the moon howls in the mysterious
Sky
As all the mums and dads get up for the
Nightshift
As all of the creatures fly around in the scary
Night sky.

The stars in the night sky are so beautiful,
In fact, the most beautiful I have ever
Seen,
In fact, they are the best stars I have
Ever seen
Because the stars in the
Land of dreams are the best stars in the
World.

Destiny Lemon (10)
Cherrywood Community Primary School, Farnborough

Dreams

Rainbows dance around my ankles,
As rivers race around me in circles,
My dreams are always with me when I sleep,
As I float on the white fluffy clouds.

Dreams fill my mind with endless thoughts,
As a magical portal knows where I will go,
Maybe dragons are rapidly racing above my clueless head,
Dreams are full of mysteries that people do not know.

Pegasus flies with light colours around them,
As I dance with happiness through the night,
Rainbow horse gallops through the sky,
Suddenly, I wake up to find all of that was just a dream.

Alice Wray (10)
Cherrywood Community Primary School, Farnborough

Nightwalker

N ight-time, cyan-like creatures lurk
I n the darkness, this creep lives
G oing to helpless houses, an ominous figure
H ell is upon them, never seen before
T hey run as if human, so silent as well
W alkers their name ends with, Night it starts
A lways mindlessly stalking poor people
L ate at night, these bad omens appear
K illers of many creatures, just awful!
E ating little animals, how carnivorous
R un when you see them, just flee!

Mailee Karim (10)
Cherrywood Community Primary School, Farnborough

Once Upon A Dream

N ight-blue sky shines,
I, at night, give hushed whispers,
G uided light shines through the windows,
H ard to sleep in the dark sky,
T he dreamy creatures come out at night,
M ild creatures roam at night,
A t the castle, I float on a cloud,
R eading the dragon news, I freeze as I turn,
E arning the sight of dark as the children doze away.

Jamie Milner (10)
Cherrywood Community Primary School, Farnborough

Strange World

As my body fell into deep sleep,
Dreams slowly crept into my mind,
Taking me to another world,
Rainbow fairies gliding up the sky,
Children dancing on the sweet grass.

A mysterious tunnel caught my attention,
As I went down the tunnel,
I fell into another universe that was different,
Rainbow pigs flying mid-air,
Waterfalls flowing out of nowhere.

Aevan Thapa Magar (9)
Cherrywood Community Primary School, Farnborough

Here Comes The Pird

Here comes the Pird
Its loud roar soars through the whole farm
The wise wrinkled Pird
The fearless guard of the sky

Here comes the Pird
Half pig, half bird
Soaring, soaring
As the protector of the sky

Here comes the Pird
Screech! Sqwark!
As it thrashes its prey
A force not to be reasoned with

Here comes the Pird
Built like a tank
Its fart is as deadly as a shark
Beware, beware of the God of Land and Sky.

George Outen (10)
Chichester Free School, Chichester

Deforestation

D eep inside the luscious land
E verywhere I walk and stand
F oliage hangs gracefully across
O rchids, ferns, vines and moss
R uby butterflies fill the air
E nergetic bees everywhere
S uddenly, trees start to fall
T urning around, I see nothing at all
A ll the beauty is now gone
T errible sights; it's all so wrong
I look at a sight as strange as can be
O nly mud lies in front of me
N ow, thankfully, I'm safe in bed, blocking out the night of dread.

Saoirse Crean (10)
Crondall Primary School, Crondall

Dreamland

Off to sleep I go
Dreaming of a rainbow
At the end a castle bright
And in it was an evil knight
My fairy and her robot friend
Chased him away
Now that's the end.

Rupert Love (9)
Crondall Primary School, Crondall

The Day I Became Famous

He was an ordinary boy, Jacob Speedo. He was walking to school near the pool and he saw a ticket for the London marathon. So all day at school he was going *zooooooom!*

So, the big day finally arrived. It was a crazy race. At first, he was tenth, out of 40,000 runners! He was going as fast as a motorbike. He was zooming past pros. He was zooming past someone to get the fastest time ever. He was second.

One mile to go! No matter what, someone was going to get the fastest time ever. He did it! The commentator shouted, "He won! Jacob Speedo, first place!" Time 1:59:59. Third was Sarah Canday. Time 2:00:01.

Sebastian Salter (9)
Downsend School, Leatherhead

Untitled

It's amazing in fantasy land. The fairies have sparkly wings and the dogs have hats. I met a fairy called Lilly and her little sister, Jose. Then we went to a fairy village. There was fairy dust everywhere. There were little houses made of love, cake and determination. They made a potion out of fairy dust to make Juliana fly. She wasn't a fairy or an elf, Juliana was an ordinary girl.
Juliana drank the potion and all of a sudden she grew wings and started flying. A few hours later the potion wore off and she fell to the floor. Suddenly she woke up, it was all a dream.

Isabella Fernandez-Pell (9)
Downsend School, Leatherhead

Infinity Dreams

Once upon a dream, I dreamt of an infinity world with no food
I was in a bad mood
Nightmares filled my head
Suddenly there were monsters scaring me

They all came towards me
I got freaked as I could see
Suddenly someone came to save me
It was a superhero

The monsters jumped with their bloody mouths
While he carried me with his helpful hands
Suddenly fireworks came booming, crashing and zooming

In the morning I woke up and looked up where my dream began
In the night sky.

Abigail Young (9)
Downsend School, Leatherhead

The Nightmare

I was settling in bed
And I fell into a nightmare.
It was dark and cold
And I didn't even know where I was
And I heard a noise.
It got louder and louder.
I saw something.
It was getting closer!
I screamed
And I was trying to get out of the dream
But the creature talked.
It said, "You are in my way."
I was scared.
I woke up with a fright
And didn't want to get out of bed.

Joseph Muller (8)
Downsend School, Leatherhead

In The Sky

I'm in the sky,
I ought to know why,
I have found this place,
With a big furry face,
I don't understand,
Even the floor is sand,
The clouds step up and down,
In this big white town,
You're upside down!
One house is a fiery feud,
The trees around it shiver in the breeze,
Almost like a big red boar,
With a hard obsidian door,
This is my house, I know,
I have to go.

Ellie Dada (9)
Downsend School, Leatherhead

Nightmares

N ight after night, I come here
I t looks like a demon playground
G rey grass
H appiness has gone
T rees are as black as a crow
M idnight has struck 12 o'clock
A t midnight the demons come and play
R un quickly or else
E veryone has disappeared
S leep is now scary.

Mae Harverson (8)
Downsend School, Leatherhead

Lucid Dreams

Sometimes nightmares haunt my sleep,
They always make me scream,
But nightmares can easily disappear,
Just say some magic words,
And then the nightmares disappear,
Lucid dreams, oh, how incredible they are.
Just go to bed and rest your head,
Remember what you have done,
As lucid dreams are amazing,
As long as you have fun!

Albie Lambert (9)
Downsend School, Leatherhead

Dreamland

Everything is upside down in dreamland,
The houses are made of delicious chocolate,
Clouds are the most fluffy luscious cotton candy,
You can hear the most beautiful cute birds chirping,
Trees dance in the distance with joy,
People can float in the air and fly like a falcon,
The air smells like amazing chocolate pizza.

Ruben Lovell-Djordjevic (9)
Downsend School, Leatherhead

Australia Dreamland

Everything is peaceful in Dreamland,
Splash went Platypus as she swam through the glistening water.
Kangaroo lay down in the shade of a beautiful tree,
She breathed in the smell of red flowers on the tree.
She saw Possum and Koala sleeping in the trees,
And went to bed with ease.

Beatrice Woolnough (9)
Downsend School, Leatherhead

Nightmares

They come to haunt your dreams,
They come to make you scream.
When they fill your head,
They also fill you with dread.

They are so bold and real,
They're like eating broccoli as a meal,
They can be about anything,
Even about a haunted king.

Ray Cummings (9)
Downsend School, Leatherhead

Waterland

Everything is water in Waterland!
You can go anywhere in Waterland, whoosh,
You can dance and prance like reindeer,
You can hear and see the water drip,
You can look at the glistening stars,
The houses are made of water, everything is!

Leo Ling (9)
Downsend School, Leatherhead

Unusual Dream

Silver shiny clouds soaring in the deep blue sky,
One carrying my dad, the other one my mum with me in the middle, together we all fly.
Angels all around us, but I am the prettiest of all,
My gorgeous mum and handsome dad doing their best to not let me fall.
Dressed up in feathers and loaded with superpowers,
We fill everyone's life with love, colours and flowers.
We keep exploring the universe from one world to the other,
Our strong bond is not short-lived but exists forever.

Sarah Locham (8)
Drove Primary School, Swindon

Monsters

Creepy little critters crawling
And scurrying under your bed
Everywhere in your room
And forgotten nightmares every night
You imagine, then boom
Lights off, all you see is loads of monsters
Monsters monsters
All you can see after dark
You fall asleep
All you can see in your dreams
Monsters can be nice but not for long...

Khadijah Mohamed (10)
Drove Primary School, Swindon

Cute Vs Scary

I woke up and what did I see?
I couldn't believe
Was I in a dream because puppies were surrounding me?
I rubbed my eyes but I didn't think it was a dream
Puppies were licking my face but I wondered why one didn't want to see me
I came over to see it
Its eyes were flashing red to white
Then it started to take flight
The others came over to see
They even fought back for me
The scary one held on tight, he lifted up all the puppies until they all took flight
The scary one grew bigger and bigger and redder and redder
Its teeth were horrifying and sharp, covered with blood
When they all thought it was about to end
All the others turned really, really cute
The scary one turned small
And he turned like all the others
All cute and cuddly

They were all best friends again
I hope they don't fall out again.

Erin Davies (9)
Drumahoe Primary School, Drumahoe

A Snorting Creature

I woke up one morning,
After the most magical dream.
There was something snorting,
Something I had never seen...
As I ran through the pink fluffy clouds,
And danced with birds,
I had never seen such a huge crowd,
When I was down on the earth.
From the corner of my eye,
I could see what was snorting,
A beautiful creature, all colours of the rainbow,
That needed a hug and needed sorting.
Its long purple hair, all glittery and pretty,
I grabbed its tiny hand and we ran away quickly.
The snorting stopped, the laughing started,
As we hopped and hopped until the time had come.
Now I wake up from that magical dream,
And we sadly parted.
I will never forget that beautiful creature,
If only I could still reach her.

Mollie Frazer (8)
Drumahoe Primary School, Drumahoe

Night Horror

N ever ever go into the forest at night or you might get a little fright
I n the forest at night, a little boy stared and said goodnight
"G oodnight!" he says. Don't say it back or you might die
H e did. I say die. I meant up to god
T o be honest I wouldn't say goodnight

H orror, it seems like you're living in a horror story
O r a nightmare, maybe you are!
R egret it now
R evenge will come tonight
O r you might die tonight
R evenge will be sought tonight.

Brooke Bradley (9)
Drumahoe Primary School, Drumahoe

Untitled

I was in a field with Phoebe randomly with Sophia's cat, Webe. There were these boys. Half of them were in my class. They were bullying us and cursing at us. I was then randomly teleported to a creepy daycare.

I was so scared. The daycare turned dark orange. Then there was a monster thingamabob that was possessed. The monster started chasing me. I almost had a heart attack.

My mum started shouting at me, saying, "Wake up, you little sleepyhead!"

Emilie King (9)
Drumahoe Primary School, Drumahoe

The Creature Knows

Something creeping in this weird place
The look of fear on my face
In a long, dark hall
A large creature begins to fall
I begin to freeze
Then fall to my knees
It's my brother
I'm glad it was no other
As the creature comes for Reuben
I hold to stop him moving
After he is taken
I smell some baking
As I follow the smell
I think I hear a bell
As I turn my head
I wake up in my bed.

Zac McGeady (10)
Drumahoe Primary School, Drumahoe

Bedtime

Off to bed, it's time to go
One, two, three, jump under the covers
As I lay my head on my fluffy pillow
The fairies start to sparkle
Scattering their magical dust
Hoping my dreams aren't full of rust
There's me, dancing in the sky
Carefree as can be, flying by
Over the stars and over the moon
I hope I don't wake up anytime soon.

Megan Hetherington (9)
Drumahoe Primary School, Drumahoe

Untitled

I was walking in the afternoon when I heard someone say, "Hey, come down. Messi and Ronaldo are playing." They were playing in the final.
"Oh yes!" I screamed.
I was so nervous to go, I even felt dizzy. All of a sudden, I was there. Don't ask me, that was a long story. It was tied by each team. It was 3-3.
In the last 4 seconds, Ronaldo scored.

Brooke McCready (10)
Drumahoe Primary School, Drumahoe

Untitled

Every night I hear monsters scratching, scraping, screeching
I see them lurking in the shadows ready to attack
But when I go to scream, everyone says, "Shh! It's just a dream!"
Their gruesome sight leaves me frozen in fear
Their glowing eyes, so bright no one hears my plea for help
My monsters whisper wicked words, their voices are parasites.

Charlie Hepburn (9)
Drumahoe Primary School, Drumahoe

In My Dreams Every Night

In my dreams every night
I see colourful clowns in sight
Running around doing tricks
Telling jokes and using magic sticks
Me and my sister did giggle
As we saw the clown doing the wiggle
We love the fair
Especially when the clown fell off the chair
Now at night I look forward to going back
As it was a really good crack.

Layla Neely (11)
Drumahoe Primary School, Drumahoe

Monsters Are Real

M any people say there aren't monsters,
O nly I know there are.
N ight after night, they give me a fright,
S caring me from near and far.
T errifying ghouls and goblins,
E nter through my bedroom door,
R eady to attack me,
S o I put some traps on the floor, and they are no more.

Eli Hunter (8)
Drumahoe Primary School, Drumahoe

Football

My dream is to become a footballer
For Man Utd
The first match was vs Liverpool
I scored ten goals
The number on my shirt was 20
My friend scored 3 goals
We won 13-0
I played upfront
It was a cup final
We were dancing in the changing room
We were singing
What a dream!

Lexie Mitchell (9)
Drumahoe Primary School, Drumahoe

Happy Things

Today I was trying to do my work. But I was daydreaming about something happy that I did. My dog, Pebbles, she kept chasing after dogs and I kept falling whilst holding her lead. Then she found a rock and she jumped into the water.

Callum Campbell (9)
Drumahoe Primary School, Drumahoe

Lost

Once upon a dream, in a place far away, lives a girl called Tamar who is scared of the dark
One night, she beams to space.

I wake up in darkness, only darkness
I fly around in darkness, then I go to a place
Then I bump into my BFF
I'm so happy
She shows me a path to the light, but then she fades away
I run away crying
In a flash, I'm gone
To a land far away

I then see a glamorous unicorn out of nowhere
It stops in my way
I jump on its back and ride to a beautiful rainbow stream

Then, behind a tree, I see my friend again
I jump to the stream
So happy am I
And I'm glad to say.

Tamar Raanan Djamal (9)
Etz Chaim Jewish Primary School, Mill Hill

What's Your Dream?

Dreams, dreams, dreams!
They always make us gleam.
You could be an astronaut,
Who explored the whole of space!
But make sure you're keeping up to pace!
You could be a dancer!
And dance with a panther!
You could be famous!
Named William Shameous!
You could be a builder!
Who hired a shielder!

But on the other side,
People are filled with pride!
You could be a brother,
Or a loving mother!
You could be a grandpa,
Who also was a band guard!
And it's all your choice.

Louis Blank (9)
Etz Chaim Jewish Primary School, Mill Hill

A Nightmare!

Shadows and spiders all over the place,
A feeling inside me shoots up to my face.

Out of the blue, I hear a door creak,
I'm frozen in fear, my head starts to freak out.

My guts have anxiety,
My brain wants to scream, my legs want to flee.

My mouth takes control and lets out a shout,
"My golly gosh, someone help out!"

I start to run, I then burst through the door,
There are people around me, I'm surrounded on the floor.

I lift up my head to see my foe,
A clown dressed in white, holding snow?

I stand my ground and throw my punch,
And what I tell you next will put you off lunch.

When I threw my punch, I found him not there,
This leaves one answer, this is a nightmare.

Oren Neidle (10)
Glebe House School, Hunstanton

After A Football Match

My legs are dead
My head is done
Where are my brain cells?
There are none.

My team wins!
Hoorah!
I am cold
I am wet.

I score
My dreams come true
The team comes running
In celebration.

I wait for them
I win the cup
I bring it home
Into the cabinet
Another trophy goes.

Wake up, Jack
Time to go!

Jack Nicholas (10)
Glebe House School, Hunstanton

Dinosaur And I Go To The Moon

One day, Dinosaur and I go to the moon,
Dinosaur and I will make it soon,
The galaxy is blue, violet and full of stars,
And the smell of the sky is like sweets and ice cream,
The stars are a place where family members lay,
And remember their family all day,
The sky is like a parent and is always there,
And the galaxy has a family of stars,
Dino's wings spread afar,
With a shimmer at the end like a twinkling star,
The stars are white, glittery chocolate bars,
The moon is cheese and ready to eat,
Finally, Dinosaur and I have made it to the moon,
So sadly, I have to say goodnight and sleep tight.

Orla Lewis (10)
Glusburn Community Primary School, Glusburn

My Worst Nightmare

N othing had prepared us for this exciting journey.
I t was a gloomy night and I was as nervous as can be.
G limpsing one side to the other, all I see is dust.
H ow in the world did I get here? I hope I can get out.
T hrashing! I saw something moving left to right.
M y life would end if anything happened to Layla.
A re you okay? A grin as big as the ocean.
R unning like a cheetah, I have to get away.
E scaping quickly out of the land.

Nina Moore (10)
Glusburn Community Primary School, Glusburn

The Dream

In my dreams, just tonight,
Different unicorns nearly took flight.
With rainbow tails and moonlit hooves,
Roaring up with a dancing groove.
Showing me the sparkling stars,
Showing me my great-grandad on Mars.
What does this mean?
Is it all a dream?
Three by three, they pass me by,
Leaving me gazing up at the sky.
Maybe someday I'll meet them again,
Wondering what I may gain.
Goodbye, dear creatures,
Thank you for showing me your features.

Ava Bond (10)
Glusburn Community Primary School, Glusburn

Surviving The Tsunami

I woke up in the morning, I opened my bedroom door,
And I was also yawning, my friend found the entrance,
But I knew it would be a long day, we went outside to play,
So I could not lie, it was an amazing day.

I would go to the biggest boat, I found a swimming pool,
I looked out my window and I saw a goat,
We went to ride slides, I was driving in my car,
And then we swam in a pool, and the journey was far,
It was very cool.

After a long time, I had an amazing day,
I finally arrived, we went back to our room.
I went inside my room, and I heard a siren,
And I saw a big broom, *and I saw a tsunami.*

I opened my suitcase, I saw a monster,
And I found a friend, it tried to help me,
I was a bit shocked to fly high,
Like a lock, I wanted to survive,
So it helped me fly.

Andrea Tertelici (8)
Goldbeaters Primary School, Edgware

My Dreams

D ancing in the cool blue water.
R unning on a colourful rainbow.
E ntering a flying pink bathtub.
A liens attacking London.
M agical, mystical fairy world.
S wimming in a lava pool.

Naba Asghar (9)
Goldbeaters Primary School, Edgware

Stacey The Shopkeeper

There once was a girl named Stacey,
Who sailed dinosaurs and dragons,
And after, she gave them to her friend, Macey,
But she would give them to her friend, Tracey,
Her best friend said, "Thank you, Stacey."

Nicole Kabuye (9)
Goldbeaters Primary School, Edgware

Nightmare

In the middle of nowhere,
I was in a room,
A bang from the door,
Bang, bang on the door,
Urgh! It's a clown,
I jumped out of the window,
On to the zipline,
Over the canyon at the end,
"At last, I got you!" said the clown,
He pushed me off,
Argh!
Wake up, or you will be late.

Drew Lord (10)
Grange CE Primary School, Grange-Over-Sands

Haunted Dreams

I have somehow appeared in a strange misty place
Suddenly a house appears, is it safe?
I run and head up to the huge oak door
Should I head in? I'm not sure
I dash in and the door locks itself
Then the lights go out, I squeal and yelp
Everything is black, am I dead?
No, I'm not, I'm at home in bed.

Reyn Gray (10)
Grange CE Primary School, Grange-Over-Sands

Awfully Awful

As I wake, I'm screaming, "No!
Wait, where am I? Oh no!"
Fully awake, I glance around,
What was that horrible crunching sound?
Looking around, I'm ready to run,
Lolling my head, this isn't much fun.
Yawning as I stretch and wake up in bed,
Awfully grateful that I am not dead.

Rowan Gray (10)
Grange CE Primary School, Grange-Over-Sands

Secrets Of The Sea

Lost in a sea of faces, clowns, painted smiles hiding tears, pirates plundering the depths.

A world of chaos and confusion where the lost wander aimlessly, seeking a light in the darkness.

The clowns dance and jest but their laughter rings hollow, their souls weighed down by sorrow.

The pirates sail on stormy seas, raiding and pillaging with greed, their hearts hardened by the chase.

In this tangled web of deceit, I search for a path to redemption, a way to escape the madness.

But the road is long and winding and the shadows grow ever darker. I make my way before it's too late.

Nadim Al Mousa (10)
Hafod Primary School, Swansea

Teachers

T alent is what teachers teach us.
E ducational lessons are provided by teachers.
A cademic teachers help us.
C urious teachers teach.
H appy teachers bring us joy.
E xisting teachers make fun lessons.
R esponsible teachers help us keep safe.
S mart teachers help us.

Esme-Rose Harris (9)
Hall Green Primary School, West Bromwich

Me, Myself

Hi, I am Akiva! My friends are cool like me.
My teachers and my family are cool like me as well.
My dad is loveable.
My mum is sensible.
My sister is cuddleable.
I can run a mile to make someone smile.
When my day comes to an end, I'll surely pray but never pretend.

Akiva Jewel Devanada (9)
Holy Cross Catholic Primary School, Liverpool

Mice Are Nice

I think mice are rather nice
Their tails are long
Their faces small
They haven't any chins at all.

Their ears are pink
Their teeth are white
They run about the house at night
They nibble things they shouldn't touch
And no one seems to like them much
But I think mice are nice.

Alberta Edosa (9)
Holy Cross Catholic Primary School, Liverpool

The Dream School Land

Once upon a dream, I was in school with everyone then at playtime, Mariana, Cecelia and I were playing together. We were so happy.
The next day, Mariana wasn't there or the next day. On Monday she was not there but on Tuesday she was.
I wasn't because I had an appointment. For lunch, I had a pizza from Wetherspoon in Clapham Junction. It was delicious. My sister also had an appointment on Tuesday. She had pasta for lunch but she didn't finish it.
Back to my friend, when she was at school there was a bomb. I only had five minutes to save her. My heart was racing so fast when I ran to save her. After five minutes I saved her. Her face was as dirty as dust. Then the bomb went *boom!*

Rebecca Laker Lebeja (8)
Holy Ghost Catholic Primary School, Wandsworth

A Head Full Of Goals

When I go to bed
I lay down my head
And surprise surprise
When I close my eyes
Football fills my head

Bed should be for sleeping
But not if you are keeping
Your favourite team from leaking
Your lead and losing the league

I'm in my bed, I'm snoring
But in my head, I'm scoring
I run from the back
Like a black ninja cat
My terrifying attack
Makes defenders strike back

I skip past each defender
As they try track back,
Tackling and turning, they can't stop my attack
Because I have a terrorising attack!

Patrick Keenan (9)
Holy Ghost Catholic Primary School, Wandsworth

Bears

Last night, I had a nightmare,
But there wasn't anything scary, not even a bear!

I'm afraid of bears; they are my worst fear,
Like a dagger, their roar hits my ear.

But bears get scared too, obviously from big things,
Like motorbikes circling them in rings.

When that scenario happens, the bear's hair stands on end,
But there is no one there to help him, so the bear must defend!

Sophie Russell (8)
Holy Ghost Catholic Primary School, Wandsworth

Once Upon A Dream

In my mind
Day and night
A magic world
Shines so bright
Am I dreaming
About this world again tonight?
Twirling and jumping
On the soft clouds
I feel sensations of freedom
While singing aloud
I want to live this life nice and proud
For what it counts I am the queen here now!

Carolina Isaza de la Rocha (8)
Holy Ghost Catholic Primary School, Wandsworth

Candyland

Have you ever been to Candyland?
Where the sky is pink not blue,
And there is glitter on poo!

Bunnies go hop, hop, hop,
And popcorn goes *pop, pop, pop!*
In Candyland, there are unicorns, dragons and fairies,
And rainbows that taste like cherries.

And don't forget all the sweet candy,
But don't eat that much or your mum will get angry!
Lollipops are as big as towers,
Which the wizards sit on and use their powers.

To bring me to Candyland every night,
Which you can find by following knights to the light.

Reeda Faizi (8)
Kingswood Primary School, Lambeth

The Ordeal Doll

The doll crept closer,
I walked further,
The doll glided across the floor like a professional surfer.
I kicked it on the floor, then ran,
The doll had hair like a lion's mane,
She had a sword as long as a cane,
I ran like I was in first place in a race,
But I tripped over my lace,
Circus music faded past my ear,
I couldn't see anything, nothing was clear.

My friend came near,
And then I had no fear,
I had a tear,
Something felt near,
I glanced at a tree with joy,
And so did my friend Roy,
Then someone lifted me on his horse,
I glared at his dark brown cape,
And then nothingness.

Takudzwa Mukozho-Sonwil (10)
Lapal Primary School, Halesowen

The Nightmare

Pure black covered the floor,
Is it a dream?
Or is it more?
How will I know?
Because it seems very strange.

Lights flicker on,
Now I know where I am,
In a small cage,
In a tiny corner,
In a big house,
How did I get here?

I gaze ahead,
To see a clown,
With a whip or a rope,
I don't know because of my frown,
That won't disappear from my face.

To my side I see,
Jamie, my brother,
Josie, my cousin,
And Tom, my friend,

Their faces painted with fear,
Just like mine.

Should I stay? Should I go?
I don't know.
Now my feet are frozen to the floor,
Should I ignore?
Or is he poor?

There is a dog in my view
Holding a small toy,
The clown's dog, or not?
It looks so vicious with sharp teeth.

Suddenly, I wake up.
Was it a dream?
I think it was
But I'm not sure.

Sophie Anderson (10)
Lapal Primary School, Halesowen

Once Upon A Dream

Through the mud
And up the stairs
I drank out of my mug
As I watched the bears

I got out of bed
And bumped my head
I heard a weird sound
So I frowned

I saw pitch black
As a clown put me to sleep
Eyes watched mouth widened
As spiders climbed over me

Floating through a pillow of clouds
Old memories of the past flew by
I went to grab them
But they dripped through my hands
Like a water fountain

I tried to run but my legs were ice
My eyes were pink marbles
As I twisted and spun
Cotton candy fell into my mouth

I gazed at the sky
As I got on a ride
An amazing world but not as it seemed
As I touched the lollipops that were curled

My head was spinning like a screw
As the sweet popcorn melted in my mouth
I was dancing like a ballerina
As I was turning south.

Maisie Williams (10)
Lapal Primary School, Halesowen

Weird Dreams

Dreams are weird.
Very weird.
Once I saw a sea of beans,
In my bathtub.

But today, my bathtub was gone!
I checked everywhere,
The kitchen,
The garden,
But then I saw it on the roof!

I climbed the roof but then,
A teddy bear pounced at me,
I jumped on the bath and it started to fly.

The bear ran as I steered it back.
Well, that was weird,
What's next?

Hashim Ahmed (10)
Lapal Primary School, Halesowen

Theme Park Tree

As the entrance grows
Like a tree from the ground
And a burger to eat tastes like a leaf
With a speedy roller coaster

A drop tower
Bigger than a tree
And a roller coaster surrounding it
Almost like a leaf

A roller coaster with loops
With a water ride
And a big Ferris wheel
With a helter-skelter.

Larry Logan (10)
Lapal Primary School, Halesowen

Monster World

M eet the Monster World
O nce upon a dream, there were lots of monsters
N one of them ever ate a human, they were scared
S ome of the monsters scared them away, but only one thing...
T hey are scared of water and fire
E very month, people come with a drink full of water so they run away
R eally, don't go, the story is getting to the scary part

W hat a day! Crazy stuff has been happening
O h really, I'm letting you know, monsters have gone missing
R onda and Londa are twin monsters, but they're missing
L ong time ago, no one has come to the Monster World
D onna the owner of the place has also gone. Or has she...?

Scarlett Du-Cille (8)
Lea Forest Primary Academy, Kitts Green

Light In The Dark

When I close my eyes,
I can see,
The sky is blue,
The grass is green,
Life isn't perfect,
But at least I have you,
Life isn't easy,
Life is hard,
Sometimes stuff is hard to discard,
Some people have jobs,
Some people have cars,
Some people think life is always hard,
But there is a peek of light in the dark,
Close your eyes,
Don't be scared,
Just stay calm,
In your dreams,
There is always a peek of light in the dark.

Laila Peace (10)
Lea Forest Primary Academy, Kitts Green

Magical World

In a faraway land,
Pink dragons and unicorns roamed in the pink sky.
You could hear a marching band.
Eating cotton candy pies that splashed and spluttered in your eyes.
Rainbows appeared from behind magical clouds.
Please come along if you're allowed.
If you ever want to visit, close your eyes and dream.
By the cotton candy houses, you will see multicoloured berries and violet flowers.
This is where you will find me!

Lyla Black (7)
Lea Forest Primary Academy, Kitts Green

The New Footballer

F ouls
O ffside
O nside
T op bins
B all
A club
L ines
L ong shot.

Adebayo Mandela Soyelu (8)
Loxdale Primary School, Bilston

In A Dream

Once upon a time, there was a little girl called Jamie. She was stuck in a dream. It was a whole story. A few minutes later, the dream started. The poem started here. I have a dream!
That I can be a leader for change,
That my family can help others succeed,
That my friends can get along better,
Oh, I have a dream...
That all children have enough to eat,
That grown-ups will stop fighting,
That people will start taking care of the Earth!
Oh, I have a dream...
That people will find peace in this world,
That people will learn how to stop fighting,
That there will be peace for all people of the world.

Daria Bargaoanu (10)
Meryfield Primary School, Borehamwood

Dancing Delight

In my dreams, all the time
I'm a ballerina, in my prime
Twirling gently, on tips of toe
Under lights that gently glow

My tutu flutters, airy and light
As I leap with all my might
The music swells a flowing tide
With each pirouette, I glide

Around the stage, my dance unfolds
In silken slippers, grace I hold
The audience fades, just the dance and me
In this world of ballet, I'm free

In my dreams, I spin, no end in sight
With every turn, my soul takes flight
A ballerina's dream, pure and divine
In the night, where the stars align.

Elsie (10)
Meryfield Primary School, Borehamwood

If I Could Fly

I would be able to touch the sky,
F ree as a bird, I'd be.

I f I could fly, I would fly around the world.

C ountries I would visit near and far,
O ver seas and oceans, I'd go,
U nder branches of trees and over the Empire State Building,
L oads of places to visit,
D eserts and mountains, what a wonderful world!

F lying is fun,
L et's glide around the world,
Y ellow sunsets and sunrises, I'd see!

Krish Singh (10)
Meryfield Primary School, Borehamwood

Flying

People having fun soaring
Through the bright, blue sky
I really want to do it
I really want to fly

I start falling down
I feel really scared
I land on my feet
I think that I am spared

I fly with my wings
I am high in the air
They get quite dirty
I don't really care

Beep! Beep! Beep!
I open my eyes
Turns out it was a dream
I'm really surprised.

Radhika Tanwar (8)
Meryfield Primary School, Borehamwood

Player Two

I see myself being bright
But at some point
Running and not scoring,
I missed and it was so annoying
One after another, I missed
I must persist.
I'm such a loser,
I just want to be proud
I have to show how good I can be
Why can't they see?
There will always be a next time
But when will it be the right time?
Player Two will lose,
Miss after miss, became a twist.

Brooklyn (9)
Meryfield Primary School, Borehamwood

Football Fan

F reddy loves football dreams,
O kay, and he also likes match dreams.
O r having a dream with a star,
T he ball has come on,
B rilliant kick he made
A nd got a goal.
L ionel Messi was there,
L osing team shook hands.

F reddy loved it!
A nd he woke up happy,
N ever had a nightmare again.

Teddy Shuttleworth (10)
Meryfield Primary School, Borehamwood

I See A Rainbow

I see a rainbow of colours way up, way up high
Long, long lines of colours bent across the sky
I can paint a rainbow, paint it with my
Hands up and over, up and over and down
Across land, first comes red and orange
Then yellow and green, last comes blue
And purple colours I have seen.

Dhrumi Patel (9)
Meryfield Primary School, Borehamwood

Dancer

D iana was a young girl who loved dancing
A t mid-day, she would start prancing
N o, she never did stop
C ause she couldn't stop through all the o'clocks
E ven when she was sad
R ather, she would never be bad!

Elisa (8)
Meryfield Primary School, Borehamwood

Lively London Dies Tonight!

Lively London here we come
Super Sumaiya is on the way
Amazing Aaminah scoots the way
Talented Tania talks her way
And happy Haleemah hops her way.

As we leave our train
Comes a man who looks in dismay
He is wearing a dress, is this a mistake?
Let's run away!

We are running for our lives
What if we see a knife?
But then a man pops out
With flyers of the Olympics, we are struck with doubt
We are filled with fear
But have time to accept this offer while we're here
The man is gone without giving our flyers
Even though we are his buyers
What a day, I have to say!

Amelia Khan (10)
Nether Edge Primary School, Sheffield

The Dream That Became My Dream!

I'm in London with my best friends and there are flying cars and they're not normal cars - they can fit one hundred people in them!
Then my friends and I ask someone, "What year is it?"
The lovely lady says, "3000."
"Is it?!" My friends and I squeal.
Then the nice old lady says, "What's up, lovely?"
"Oh nothing," Betty, Amelia, Scarlett and I say.
So my friends and I go for a walk around for a bit and we see people teleporting.

Josie Slaler-Winter (10)
Newtown CE (VC) Primary School, Gosport

Untitled

I am in my Xbox room,
Now I'm all alone,
I wish I was playing with my friends,
I will always have an Xbox room.

Oscar Usher (10)
Newtown CE (VC) Primary School, Gosport

Football

In fields of green where dreams take flight,
A 9-year-old with all his might,
Grasps his football, full of zeal,
Ready to conquer, ready to feel.

His tiny hands, they grip so tight,
As he takes off into the light,
With every step, a world anew,
His passion burns, his spirit true.

Through grassy plains and dusty ground,
He dribbles, dances, hears the sound,
Of cheering crowds inside his head,
As he imagines the goals he'll spread.

He dreams of matches grand and tall,
Where he's the hero, standing tall,
With every kick, a goal he'll score,
His heart's ambition, evermore.

For in his world of pure delight,
A 9-year-old with all his might.
Plays with joy, his spirit bright,
Guided by his football's light.

Ismael Abbas (10)
Norfolk House School, Edgbaston

Nightmare

Once upon a dream,
I was sleeping peacefully, then a knock on my bedroom door,
I thought it was my mum, but in fact it was a group of spiders,
Deadly spiders,
I ran and ran for my life,
What if I don't have a life?
Scary things happen to my life,
While dark, misty skies fall down to a sunset,
A lightning struck my head,
I was feeling so good that I fell asleep,
In my dream, spiders come crawling up my head,
For some reason, I feel like Spider-Woman,
My face is turning black and my eyes red,
What is happening to me?

Sergi Tasali (9)
Oak Lodge Primary School, West Wickham

Dive In

Dedicated to my little sister who never gives up and always achieves her dreams!

When I jump in, I sink,
Do it again, the same thing,
I try again, but can barely breathe,
The next day, I go back in,
One leg I kicked,
The next day another,
Added in the arms,
At last, I became a swimmer.

Maisie Willsmore (10)
Oak Lodge Primary School, West Wickham

Dreams Of The Sun

The sun is always smiling
And it has a very big mouth
And it is very bright
And it is very round and spiky
And it feels smooth and silky
And it dreams very big, good dreams
And the sun is happy and nice
And the sun shines like a bright rainbow
And its eyes shine like diamonds
And it flies up high.

Charlie Carew (9)
Pontarddulais Primary School, Pontarddulais

Dreams

D o good in life.
R un through the clouds.
E at the clouds like they're cotton candy.
A re you good in life or not?
M agic comes from dreams.
S ometime, you will find your way in life.

William Stevens (9)
Pontarddulais Primary School, Pontarddulais

Untitled

R ugby, I love the game
U nder the bar, I score
G reat teamwork
B elieving I'll fulfil my dreams
Y es, one day I'll play in the Principality Stadium.

Jake Gabe (9)
Pontarddulais Primary School, Pontarddulais

Candy City

This morning I woke up
I brushed my teeth with a gingerbread toothbrush
And frosting toothpaste
My gingerbread dog came in
I'm also a gingerbread girl
I put my KitKat dress on
I went downstairs and had breakfast
It was cotton candy cereal
And then I went onto the gingerbread bus
And talked to my friends
Finally, we made it to school
First class, I had maths, English and singing
Next up was lunch
I had a jam sandwich and a yoghurt with a candyfloss drink
After lunch, we went outside, and after that, we had science, PSHE and art
Then I went home on the gingerbread bus
Finally, high school was done
I put my PJs on
I was on my iPhone until 8:30pm
Then I finally went to sleep
Goodnight, dog.

Ruby-Mae Evans (9)
Provost Williams CofE Primary School, Coventry

Deep Sleep Nightmares

I was alone,
In a dark, dark field.
About to go into a pitch-black forest.
There were ghosts roaming in circles around me.
Then I got a cold shiver.
It went down my spine,
Because my biggest fear,
Was right behind me.
It was loads of creepy dolls.
They were all prancing around me,
With all of the ghosts.
Then I walked forward, confused,
Into the dark forest.
The ghosts followed, and so did the dolls.
I was getting anxious,
Nervous, and scared.
Then I felt another shiver
Down my spine
It was very cold
Colder than the last time
I was scared because
I felt a hand, it was on my back…
Then the next thing that happened was

I was in a measureless sleep
When I awoke
I was in a murky room
With the ghostly dolls and haunting ghosts
But they said, "Escape"
Then they were gone
There were lots of different clues
I didn't know where to start
But then I saw the clues
Had numbers on
I looked for the number one
It was hidden well
I completed the task
It was to write a poem
Then I did the rest quick
Because it was easy peasy
Then on number ten
Was the key
It was the key to escape
I jogged to the door and I escaped
I dashed down the hallway and down the stairs
And out through the front door
Then I sprinted and ran for my life
Then I woke up in my bed
Feeling full of dread.

Olivia Summers (8)
Provost Williams CofE Primary School, Coventry

My Dark Nightmare

D eep in darkness, it watches me,
A re you my dark end?
R ed demon eyes, deep black cloak,
K iller in disguise, what happens now?

N early dawn, it grabs me, screeching.
I nstead of screaming, I fight,
G etting closer to my short fate; I am saved.
H igh in the moonlight, a white angel nears,
T eeth are bared, good and bad fight.
M eeting their matches.
A ngel prevails, night falls and light rises.
R eading out, I plead, "Please, what is this?"
E ntranced all night, I wake in the morning, still wondering if my saviour will ever come back...

Kaitlyn Martin (11)
Rackenford CE (VA) Primary School, Rackenford

Night

Now as the night approaches,
I'm outside my house,
I hear a roar!
Up in the sky when I discover...

In the dark misty air,
I discover a floating island,
It's dancing in the sky waiting for me to go up,
I'm as confused as a dog searching for his ball.

Going up the zipline, I see everything upside down,
And hundreds of monsters all around,
I specifically see a brick monster,
He's a ground shaker.

High in the sky,
The big, brown brick monster,
It's glaring at me,
I'm scared!

"Time for school," my mum says,
I wake up,
Phew! It was a dream!

Rosie Webber (9)
Rackenford CE (VA) Primary School, Rackenford

Magic Palace

Magic in the air, potions everywhere
In a palace full of magic, so many explosions, loud and big
Penny, Lucia, Scarlett and Talia
We danced a happy jig
The aliens were friendly with smiles bright and wide
We played games and had fun
No need to run and hide.

Penny Clarke (8)
Sacred Heart Catholic School, Thornton-Cleveleys

Railway Train

R *ump, rump!* My heart went, beeping as fast as an alarm
A ll there was, silence in the train, time travelling slowly
I awoke, suddenly, the train drifting through the railway
L aughing siblings, about a haunting joke, terrified, my eyes
W olf howling away in the middle of nowhere, howling leader
A swaying train, slowly moving
Y elping dogs waiting for help

T *ick, tick,* the clock went, time went by
R umbling train passing by
A *woo, awoo!* The wolf howled as loud as thunder
I gnoring sisters, waiting to go to sleep
N ow time flies, sitting here, bored.

Chiara Lock (12)
Shobdon Primary School, Leominster

Time Travel

In my dream,
A time machine,
Travelling in time
Would be fine,
I need to make
The perfect rhyme,
Before I travel in time.

Saffire Crick (10)
Shobdon Primary School, Leominster

An Outcast Dragon

A small door opened, a hole in the wall,
A huge beam of colour, I was enthralled,
Dragons of all colours, red, green and blue!
I was shocked, this was all so new!
But as I looked to the shadows, I turned round to see,
A black, colourless dragon, an outcast he may be.
All the other dragons laughed and called him names,
Because he was scaly, and they all had manes.
'Trouble' and 'dangerous', that's what they'd all say,
But the dragon was gorgeous, sparkling in the light of the day.
A whip of his tail and fire that caused fright,
All the smoke cleared and he was black and white.
Checkered like a chessboard from nose to tail,
Even the end sparkled on his nail!
He was so pretty, better than the rest,
Even he knew now that he was the best.

Sienna Dent-Sheath (13)
St Bede's Catholic Academy, Ashby

Once Upon A Dream

Once upon a dream,
Every night, all I dream about is marrying
A dreamy dreamer, a man called Jota.
His eyes sparkle like twinkly stars.
His hair feels like a freshly groomed dog.
His skin feels as smooth as silk.

My dream feels that real that I feel
Like I can hold him in my arms.
My dream feels so real that it feels like
He is with me
As I go through my day
All I can think of is my Jota.

Keeley Woodmansey (12)
St Bede's Catholic Academy, Ashby

Mysterious Match

Once upon a dream, I am in a mysterious match
And my teacher is here, and my friends
And I guess it is a school trip...
There are people cheering
And the ball glides.

Azim Sidiqi (9)
St Clare's Catholic Primary School, Bradford

Nightmare: Losing A Friend

Nothing like this has happened before.
I saw my friend standing sad and alone.
Glaring at me with sadness in her eyes.
"Hi," I said. "What a nice surprise."

Then she was shouting at me like I hurt her.
She screamed, "Ella's coming, leave me alone!"
Maybe I'd done something wrong.
Thoughts rushed through my head.
What have I done?
Is she okay?

All of a sudden, my friend, Ella, came from nowhere.
Running away before my eyes.
Everywhere, all dull and dark.

All of a sudden, I woke up, all comfy in my bed,
With my mum kissing my head.
"Good night," she said.

Chloe Hale (12)
St Edward's CE Academy, Leek

This Doesn't Seem Right

When I woke up, bright
Something didn't feel right
When I went down the stairs
I only got weird stares
When I looked at the couch
It opened with a grouch
When I got sucked into a hole
I saw I was in a big bowl
Then a crowd arrived
I realised I was inside
A beautiful football pitch
After a long day, I had a big stitch
And then I heard my name
Then I rose to fame
Out of my bed
And then I said
"Five more minutes, Mum!"

Oscar Budd (12)
St Edward's CE Academy, Leek

Euros

E ngland will win the EURO – the trophy of the year
U nder the heat, teams will tremble in fear
R umble will the crowd when Kane scores again
O ver and over, England fans will cheer
S tronger and stronger, we come back each year.

Gabe Ager (12)
St Edward's CE Academy, Leek

Dream

S ometimes I dream
L ike it seems real
E ven the imaginary ones that can never happen
E ven the signs that have been seen
P lease dream, don't leave!

Jack Siwiec (12)
St Edward's CE Academy, Leek

Once Upon A Dream

I saw a lion, fierce and strong,
Prowling, prowling, prowling.
When she is hungry
All she wants is meat, meat, *meat!*
I freeze and watch in fear,
There is no meat.
Just flowers, flowers, flowers.
The lion sniffs, sniffs, sniffs.
She smells the sweet flowers,
And rolls, rolls, rolls.
I saw a lion playful and happy.

Felicity Robinson (9)
St James' CE Primary School, West End

A Trip To Legoland

At night when I am asleep
Into my dreams I creep
I dream about travelling here and there
I dream about travelling everywhere
Tonight I'm travelling to Legoland
Full of excitement, ticket in hand

We head for the rides
My eyes open wide
The rides give me a thrill
But suddenly I get a chill
As I look down
I see a clown
His face is full of glee
But I find him really creepy
I jump off the ride
And run and hide
I hide in Miniland
Where the builds are so grand
But as I look around I see, it's in disarray.

Alfie Li (10)
St John's CE Primary School, Keele

Achieve Your Dreams

Achieve your dreams
It's not hard
But you need to put your mind to it
And you need to focus on it
If not, you will lose sight of your goal
You should not let them fade away.

Achieve your dreams
Don't let anyone stop you from doing it
It might not be easy to succeed
But you need to put effort in and try
Because that's the way you will become a shooting star.

Achieve your dreams
You shouldn't do it because someone tells you to
You should only do it because the inside of you tells you to do it.

Oleena Kabbekadaurs (9)
St John's CE Primary School, Keele

Unicorns Are Friends

Unicorns bouncing through the sky
They were going so high
In the fantasy land, the three unicorns spotted two girls
Their names were Autumn and Sage
The playful unicorns came from backstage
Autumn stroked the unicorns
The unicorns laid down their horns
To say welcome
Sage and Autumn were taken along the world for a trip
After going on a trip they were in shock
They wanted to go get their suitcase and start to knock
The unicorns eventually asked them to stay
The girls took the invitation and they were so happy.

Olivia Abbotts (10)
St John's CE Primary School, Keele

Dreams

Dreams can be good,
Dreams can be bad,
Dreams can be happy,
Dreams can be sad,
Some dreams might be feared,
But my dreams are just weird,
No matter how hard I try,
No matter if I ask myself why,
I just keep dreaming of goats,
Yes, you heard right,
All day and even night,
I dream of goats,
Some girls dream of shoes, some girls of coats,
But not me, I dream of goats,
As soon as I fall asleep,
Not cows, not even sheep,
Not a fancy holiday, not even a big boat,
Just a goat.

Ella-Rose Richardson (9)
St John's CE Primary School, Keele

The Enchanted Forest

As I drifted off in my bed
I felt a rather strange feeling in my head
Suddenly, I saw a beautiful forest
Out of all the places I've been to
This was the darkest
All I could see was the midnight moon
That lit up the inky black darkness
Little did I know what would happen soon.

A small creature rushed up to me
Covered in icy frost
But I couldn't pay attention to it
Since I was filled with exhaustion
I felt my eyes slowly lifting open
And here I am safe in my own room.

Aarha Haider (10)
St John's CE Primary School, Keele

Fairy Lost In Candy Land

C andy Land is amazing!
A ctually, in Candy Land, there is a fairy.
N o one dirty is allowed in Candy Land.
D id you know Candy Land makers allow fairies?
Y es, Candy Land is made of cream.

L illy, a Candy Land maker, is a fairy herself
A nd you are not allowed to wear black.
N o one is allowed in Candy Land without a sweet tooth.
D id you know Candy Land makers are not allowed in Candy Land?

Renee Wilcox (8)
St Joseph's Catholic Primary School, Kirkham

I Want To Be An Ice Princess

I want to be an ice princess,
I want blonde, wavy hair,
I want a blue and lilac, sparkly dress,
I want a giant blue castle, with an ice rink in my garden,
I want blue ice skates with gold butterflies on them,
I want to be with my friends and family,
And live in a small village by the sea.

Bonnie Rees (10)
St Mary's Catholic Primary School, Preston

The Magical Monster

When I ride my bike, or go on a hike,
Something feels strange.
I feel I'm being followed,
By a being, close in range.
I don't know what's behind me,
So I wouldn't dare to look around though.
I turn around to find...
A friendly, massive, magical monster!

Leo Arnold (9)
St Mary's Catholic Primary School, Preston

Dough

I rolled the dough,
In the oven it goes.
I wanted pepperoni, Mum said, *"No!"*
I just had cheese.
Mum asked if I wanted peas.
I shouted, *"No, I want pepperoni, please!"*

Charlie Roberts (9)
St Mary's Catholic Primary School, Preston

Zombies

In my dream, I ran away from zombies
And I ran fast and I found houses
I looked out of the window, I could see trees
But one scene later, zombies came. I said, "Help, zombies!"

Three months later, I'm happy because the zombies died
On Monday, I was in my house playing with my friend, Mered
But only last week, zombies came from a scary house
I ran fast like a Lamborghini and I saw a police bus

The zombies came, I had to run away
I ran miles throughout the day
They ran so fast but I saved myself
Oh, some of the dead zombies are scary

Zombies came back to the house
This time, the mice were zombie mice!
They smelt so bad, their flesh was decaying
Some zombie children were playing and skipping.

Umut Uras Gokpinar (9)
St Mary's CE Primary School, Barnsley

Unicorns

In my dream, I was riding a rainbow unicorn,
My unicorn had a sparkly horn,
Zoom! My unicorn was flying in the sky,
Everyone else asked me why!

The unicorn liked to have its hair brushed,
That is why it looked so nice and lush!
The unicorn's favourite drink is slush,
After he drinks it, he becomes all mush!
His mane is very soft and long,
As he has it brushed, he likes to sing a song,
The song he sings is so sweet,
It would make you all weep!

Then it is time to fly,
I am so excited, I feel like I could cry!
As we take off into the sky,
I take this chance to wave goodbye!

Ella Knighton (9)
St Mary's CE Primary School, Barnsley

Upside-Down World

In my dreams the world is upside down,
This is strange and makes me frown.
The trees are upside down and look like soldiers,
The clouds look like boulders.

As I walk I hear a pop.
I have to look and stop.
As I walk, the green sky touches my head,
I have to look ahead.

It seems strange to see that the birds are not in the sky,
I cannot tell a lie!
You must be careful not to go near the sun.
As you could get burnt, and that won't be fun.

Instead of cars, people drive aeroplanes.
No more cars or even trains!
The air is clean and feels really fresh,
It makes the world feel less stress.

Adeline Moore (9)
St Mary's CE Primary School, Barnsley

Darts World

The dartboard was as hard as a rock,
But was not shaped like a block.
As I wandered around the stadium floor,
I bumped into a silly door.

Inside the stadium, I could smell rubber,
I was so excited, it made me shudder.
Beneath my feet, the ground was hard,
It was a funny sight because the darts were made from card.

Around me, people were playing darts,
Around me, there was a dog that barked.
Quickly, I wanted to start,
Therefore, I picked up a dart.

The stadium was very loud,
There was a massive crowd.
The dartboard was colourful,
Darts World was wonderful.

Rafe Trickett (8)
St Mary's CE Primary School, Barnsley

Fire Land

In my dream, the world is made of fire,
I cannot help but admire.
As I walk, my feet get hot,
I start to lose the plot!

Everywhere is so orange and red,
I must be careful where I tread!
In the distance,
It looks like there is no existence.

Suddenly, I can see a fire unicorn,
I can eat lots of popcorn.
In the distance, there is a castle,
I want to go to it, but it seems a hassle.

Flames reach high, they feel so hot,
Just like a nasty witch's pot.
The fire does a freaky dance,
I need to escape; this is my last chance!

Carla Wilson (8)
St Mary's CE Primary School, Barnsley

Candy Land

In my dreams, I ate watermelon sours,
It made me have special powers,
I dreamt that I made a cake,
I had to have help to bake.

I dreamt that the clouds were fluffy,
Then I could fly like the character Buffy,
I ate some sweets, and my mouth went pop,
The sweets were so yummy, I couldn't stop.

There was ice cream, creamy and cold,
I needed to have a hold,
It looked so tasty and smelled so good,
Could I have a taste? I think I should!

James Long (9)
St Mary's CE Primary School, Barnsley

Magical Football Wonderland

In my dream, I am in space
It is a crazy place
All day we are playing football
Until the crowd begins to brawl!

I play for the mighty reds,
We have our own beds,
I wake up, I am very happy,
I am one happy chappie!

I play a thousand games,
I am now in the Hall of Fame,
I saw a lion with a crazy mane,
It even had a crazy name!

There was a food stall, the food was very nice,
I had a drink that had lots of ice,
There was a bakery with lots of cake,
I wonder how much they have to bake?

Charlie Dutton (9)
St Mary's CE Primary School, Barnsley

My Dream

Floating houses high up in the clouds,
The people were flying,
No school for one year,
The cars are flying,
I want to be a footballer,
I wish I was a gamer.

Seb Jarocki (9)
St Matthew's CE Primary School, Blackmoor

The Horrible Wizard

There once was a horrible wizard named Harry
Harry was a very unkind person
He was so crazy he put a spell on my friend Maxi
We were hiding behind the books that smelt like an old man's feet!
When he ran over we both thought it was over!
This castle was gargantuan, we thought he was never gonna find us!
But he found us and we just thought, *run!*

JJ Finnegan (10)
St Modwen's Catholic Primary School, Burton-On-Trent

Space Travel

I am flying in a rocket on a starry night,
The galaxy is so bright,
The height of the rocket is so high.

I hear a sound like *swoosh*,
I land on the moon soon,
I'm enjoying it, "Woo hoo!"

I explore way more,
I don't talk, just go further,
Still, I don't talk, I am in awe.

Raphael Chacko (10)
St Modwen's Catholic Primary School, Burton-On-Trent

Nightmares, Nightmares, I Hate Nightmares

N ew dreams every day
I ce Cream Land is everything I can see
G reat ice cream house, lovely just for me
H igh above I can see an ice cream, it's lovely for me
T he beautiful ice cream is looking at me
M y ice cream is really cold
A lovely big juicy ice cream, I love it
R ight, I need some ice cream
E very day I love ice cream
S ometimes I can't have ice cream sadly.

Ariah Nable-Russell (8)
St Peter's Catholic Primary School, Dagenham

While I Was Dreaming

D reaming softly, tucked up warm.
R ude monsters entered my bedroom.
E mptying all my drawers out onto the floor.
A gain and again and again.
M um coming! Quickly hide!
I nto the cupboard, *destroy destroy!*
N ow let's leave! *Ha ha ha.*
G oing out the window quietly. *Click.*

Orla O'Dwyer (9)
St Peter's CE Primary School, Chorley

Amazing Superpowers

Time to go to bed,
Hopefully, I don't have to dread,
I want it to be nice,
This wand is magical, just magical,
Nothing scary,
Just fairies,
Lots of cold places,
Brrr!
There's dancing,
Plants prancing,
Wahoo!
Even superpowers!
I can fly!
This whole dream is like a superpower.
I hope this can be forever and forever,
A couple of minutes later
I see a beautiful rainbow.
Uh-oh! Time to go!
Now it's over,
But it was incredible,
Just incredible!
I feel motion sick,

Probably from flying,
Wooo!

Joseph Dean (8)
Staynor Hall Community Primary Academy, Selby

Untitled

The clown is singing,
There will be a goal in the air later.
The clowns are waving,
There will be a magic trick in the air later.
A fairy is acting,
There is magic under the chairs on Friday.
The fairies are dancing,
There is a wand in space on Tuesday.
A fairy is dancing,
There will be wings on a different planet on Friday.
The footballer is wearing a crown in space on Tuesday.
The clown is dancing,
He has a crown on his head in the morning.

Janusz Bowes (8)
Staynor Hall Community Primary Academy, Selby

The Space Cat

Space cat, space cat, flying all around!
Space cat, space cat, with his helmet on!
Space cat, space cat, flying next to the sun!
Space cat, space cat, having the most fun on the sun!
Space cat, space cat, is as fluffy as a cloud!
Space cat, space cat, meows but with no sound!
Space cat, space cat, can he walk at all?

Ruby Liddle (9)
Staynor Hall Community Primary Academy, Selby

When My Plants Ran Away

One day I was carrying seeds,
And when I put them down
My plants ran away to
Poland, and stayed there
For a thousand weeks and
By then I was 73 years old
And I was happy that my plants
Came back.

Jason Samson (8)
Staynor Hall Community Primary Academy, Selby

Space

The clown is doing a handstand in the stars of space. On Friday, a fairy is dancing in a spaceship! The footballer is playing on a different planet.

Patrick Bowes (8)
Staynor Hall Community Primary Academy, Selby

Winter Wonderland

Every night, when I fall asleep,
I find myself in a wonderful land.
I walk past to see wizards
Casting magnificent spells
To help fairies, a fairy school.
They wave at me when I pass by,
Fairies flying from shop to shop.
When I heard a scream,
I immediately ran to the castle.
I found out the Royal Family was gone!
They said that after the youngest had blown the candles of her birthday cake,
All of the Royal Family just... disappeared!
The entire town was looking for them for a week.
By now, not in the deep, dark forest.
I went looking in there.
I found them.
I asked what they were doing here.
The youngest said she wished to go
Where she grew up with family!
I woke up to find out that I just had a dream... or did I?

Holly Bonner (9)
Tany's Dell Primary School & Nursery, Harlow

Untitled

There was a little boy called Chace Brown and his lost friends called Aronas, Zayne, Teddy, Jaxon, Ali and Archie. Sadly, their parents abandoned them. They saw a very big boat. They were on a very small island so they made their way to the boat to the ocean at night. They slept, they forgot they were in the boat. They were stranded! They started to sail to any island. It took them two weeks.

They finally found an island with a bunch of people. They got a job then they got money. They had enough to buy football kits and a football. They practised and a football scout watched them then. They got signed up for Man City. They of course accepted. It was Chace's favourite team and they got a tonne of money.

Chace Brown (8)
Tany's Dell Primary School & Nursery, Harlow

Clowns

There was a clown in the park in the night.
There was no light, it was pitch black.
We stood still like a statue.
It started to move.
We didn't know what to do, it went *boo!*
Grayson and Skylah said, *"Argh!"*
We got knocked out.
We woke up! It was just a dream!

Davina Bonsu (9)
Tany's Dell Primary School & Nursery, Harlow

A Win

I can see the fire burning in my hand and a dragon next to me. I am with Jaxson George. I am feeling nervous. We are going into battle with Godzilla and Kong and Buialohta. We are going to push them in the water and win and then they go off.

Jacob Fisk (8)
Tany's Dell Primary School & Nursery, Harlow

Lots Of Superheroes

Me and my aunts are superheroes.
An asteroid came.
Whoosh!
We got the whole town to evacuate.
Luckily, no one was harmed.
We went back and lived happily ever after!

Erin Pennell (9)
Tany's Dell Primary School & Nursery, Harlow

A Spider!

There is a spider above my bed.
What if he falls on my head?
I would shout and scream.
This is my worst dream.
The spider is big and hairy.
That is why he is scary.

Ivaylo Todorov (9)
Tany's Dell Primary School & Nursery, Harlow

Dance Teacher

I have always dreamt of being a dance teacher,
I went to Cloud Land,
The children wanted to dance,
I was going to be the best teacher ever.

Alyssa Gibbons (9)
Tany's Dell Primary School & Nursery, Harlow

Untitled

I see a monster with my sister
Scared is how I feel.
Oh, oh, they will eat me.
I escape and find a way out.
"Help," I cry!

Sana Sakak (9)
Tany's Dell Primary School & Nursery, Harlow

Holiday To Tenerife

"**H** oliday to Tenerife"
O n the 3rd of August, I dreamt of going to Tenerife
L ying in the golden sun
I didn't care about anything
D own on the beautiful beach
A nd sipping a strawberry smoothie
Y ou wish to be here too.

T enerife is actually so stunning
O h, how I wish I could go back

T he beaming sun hit me
E very day, for two weeks, I was happy
N o one could take my joy away
E ven if they tried their hardest
R eality hit when...
I woke up, every bit of joy vanished
F eeling miserable, I sat up
E ven though it was all a dream.

Danielle Abbott (13)
The Friary School, Lichfield

My Dream

In my dream at night
I see starlight shining bright
Space rocks appear beaming down at the tower
Mythical dragons fly into the sky like a butterfly
Over the moon far away
Legendary butterflies wanted to play
The blue dragon flew higher and higher
And got a breathtaking view
At the end of the night
The dragon was afraid of the light
Up high there was a beautiful butterfly shining bright
Dragons wanted to fly but they were scared of the flight
Down on the ground, there was a magical apple in the tower
Dragons were flying up and up
Then saw a fire dragon breathing suns
At night the blue dragons saw a light
Then ate it with all his might
At night there was a beam of light
Shining down at the tower.

Zhen Labandero (8)
Three Bridges Primary School, Three Bridges

The Adventure Of The Abandoned Forest

Day and night
In a blizzard sight,
I heard a wizard
Who had a fright.

Ready in delight,
In the night,
There was a hut
In a rare spot.

Everyone made a hut,
Out of wood,
In the forest, there was a fog,
In a fright,
I got my light.
In my bag,
That was in sight.

On a morning that is good,
He will collect honey for his food.

Theodore C (8)
Three Bridges Primary School, Three Bridges

Halloween

In the distance lanterns lay
Over there is a pile of hay
I'm in a happy mood
To eat some yummy food.
In the garden toy flowers bloom
Later on, I see the moon.
Now it's time to trick or treat
Everybody - pick a sweet!
In the trees there are leaves
And a colony of honey bees!

Asiya Islam (8)
Three Bridges Primary School, Three Bridges

Dreams And Light

In my dreams at night
I see a little light.
The sun beams down and I see
A dragon saying hi to me.

Dragons fly at a great height
And they fly with all their might.
Dragons skipping around and getting dizzy,
Keeping themselves busy.

Daria Dadu (8)
Three Bridges Primary School, Three Bridges

Mystical Creatures And Robin Hood

In the blistering, dark, scary woods,
There was a man called Robin Hood.
Then in a woodland, my heart was pounding,
To an awful sounding.
But the awful sound was a dragon,
Deep in the woodland and far from me,
I decided to stay.

Daniel James Goncalves (8)
Three Bridges Primary School, Three Bridges

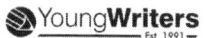

Dinosaur Dream

D inosaurs
R ule my mind
E verything I want to eat
A m I going to get eaten?
M any dinosaurs
S tegosaurus growing tiny to tall.

Adrian Fernandes (8)
Three Bridges Primary School, Three Bridges

Sparkling In The Night

In the city up above,
All stars will shine in the deep dark night,
In the bright,
In the moonlight,
In the sight.

Ricky Bindela (8)
Three Bridges Primary School, Three Bridges

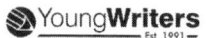

The Dangerous Dream

In my dream, a dangerous and unknown creature came out of nowhere. They all started going crazy. Then they were all gone.

Some people were in a shop drinking tea as a family but there was one friend of theirs until a guy gave the girl a small piece of a sweet. Then she started to feel weird, so she asked her parents if she could go back home.

In a blink of an eye, he was standing right at their gate. Her parents asked him why he was there. So he asked if it would be okay to charge his phone for fifteen minutes. The parents said that it would be okay, but the mum had a bad feeling about the guy. But the guy who was there was the devil, and after he gave the girl the sweet, she turned into a devil, and she would always be listening to the man. She put a song on for a long time because the man, who was a devil, told her to dance.

After a few years, the guy took the girl to his house where he tricked parents by taking their daughters, turning them into devils. They were all possessed until the girls' dads came and saved all of them and gave them back to their own parents.

Mariah Syed (9)
Upton Cross Primary School, Plaistow

Magic And Mystery

M esmerising remote island,
A bsolute mystery,
G lowing, gleaming, glistening mushrooms,
I ntriguing island,
C onquering magic.

M ysterious jellyfish,
Y ummy treats,
S uperior views,
T *hud!* A coconut crashes to the ground!
E erie eyes blink from the sky,
R ealistic,
Y aks walk on the ground.

Sheyzda Uddin (10)
Upton Cross Primary School, Plaistow

Love The Game

In my dream every night,
Footballers kick the ball and go,
Round and round and goes in the goal.
People cheering and shouting,
And going to the finals.

Ibrahim Ansar (10)
Upton Cross Primary School, Plaistow

Football And Family

Man United, Blackburn, Pompey,
We all watch with excitement on the TV
Each of us support a different team
But all follow the game, have the same dream
Me, my dad and my brother all united by the game
We all want to win the league, we all want the same.

Spencer Rolfe (10)
Victory Primary School, Portsmouth

Bugatti Veyron Wins

C ome on Bugatti Veyron
A round the tracks the cars fly
R acing for the world's best supercar trophy
S ports car race finished and my Bugatti Veyron won!

Ralph Boon (7)
Weston Turville Church Of England School, Weston Turville

When I Close My Eyes

When I close my eyes
I can see a perfect world
A world where everyone is friendly and kind
A world where there are no fears
A world where I can dance and sing.

Sometimes I can see a dog in front of me
A dog who wants to play
He wants to play all day
When you dream
You can't imagine what you'll see
A horse galloping on soft, green grass
A fish who loves sea bass.

There are so many things to see
But only if you believe.

Shh, shh, shh
Dream, dream, dream.

Estrella Dada (8)
Whitchurch Primary School & Nursery, Stanmore

Catty And Me Go On An Adventure

In my dream, Catty and I zoom off to the sun.
We always have lots of fun.
Zooming here, zooming there.
Spreading joy and happiness everywhere.
Finally, we are coming in to land,
At Willy Wonka's Chocolate Land.
Catty fell into some chocolate
And rolled in some rainbow sand.
As I started to laugh, I fell forward, where did I land?
In the rainbow chocolate sand.

Marayha Hunter-Holness (9)
Woodcock Hill Primary School, Northfield

My Castle

I wake up in my golden bed,
Which reflects off my golden window.
In my astonishing castle,
I float around my splendid bathroom.
I dance upon my golden staircase,
Glancing at the sun's reflection.

Howaida El Sanousi (9)
Woodcock Hill Primary School, Northfield

Forest Tree

Oh forest tree so bright!
Won't you guide me with your light?
Your beautiful golden leaves on the silver tree,
Many pass the forest tree filled with glee.

We pass the forest tree filled with wisdom,
As we enter your splendid kingdom.
Scattering magic across the land,
If you can hear me come hold my hand.

Under the golden sun golden apples glisten,
With beautiful birds who sing and twitter.
It was so quiet you could hear,
The morning birds roll and doze.

Suddenly, I see a bright light,
What a terrible sight.
It was all just a dream,
And I was about to enter the stream.

Nibras Ibrahem (8)
Woodhouse Primary Academy, Quinton

I Can (Pelé)

My idol Pelé says,
"You've got to pay the skills
For the bills.
You've got to put it top bins,
And smash it bottom bins."

He has unstoppable five-star skills!
In a match, sweat runs down him.
Five-star weak foot,
Costing the Galaxy...
Boom! No one can stop him.

He can shoot from miles,
With piles of money,
With new sneakers and tici taci.
Bicycle kicks and rainbow flicks,
Costing money for the famous around the world.
Like ten men's earnings for thirty years
He's the GOAT!

Monty Lewis (10)
Woolaston Primary School, Lydney

My Dream

Supercars are my whole dream,
They fly as fast as a shooting beam.
My mansion climbs in the sunlight,
My lifelong dream is in sight.

In the World Cup, I got told off by the referees,
But at least it's all good memories.
Score! goes the ball into the net, it flew so far,
This is what all my big dreams are.

Jack Clarke Wandlass (8)
Yohden Primary School, Peterlee

The Xbox Kid And Fortnite Kid

Gaming all night on my Xbox One
The sun is up before I have won
I load my gun, aim and shoot
Ranking down to diamond two
Losing more until I'm bronze 2
Next game I play with my friend Timmy
He carries me
"I'm going pro," I say
Timmy says, "Let's get unreal"
We win the World Cup, we are rich
I love Fortnite
Win the next World Cup
He says, "Stop hacking on live YouTube"
Then I carry him to a win
But he dies
64,890 times I have played,
I play Fortnite 24/7.

Teddie Davies (10)
Ysgol Y Plas, Colwyn Bay

YOUNG WRITERS INFORMATION

We hope you have enjoyed reading this book – and that you will continue to in the coming years.

If you're a young writer who enjoys reading and creative writing, or the parent of an enthusiastic poet or story writer, do visit our website **www.youngwriters.co.uk**. Here you will find free competitions, workshops and games, as well as recommended reads, a poetry glossary and our blog.

If you would like to order further copies of this book, or any of our other titles, then please give us a call or visit **www.youngwriters.co.uk**.

Young Writers
Remus House
Coltsfoot Drive
Peterborough
PE2 9BF
(01733) 890066
info@youngwriters.co.uk

YoungWritersUK   **YoungWritersCW**
youngwriterscw   **youngwriterscw**